Relativism

Mary Ford Neal

First published by Taproot Press 2022

ISBN: 978-1-8380800-0-6-8

Printed and bound by Totem Printing, Inowrocław, Poland

Typeset in 11 point Garamond by Main Point Books, Edinburgh

For my mother

Poems previously published elsewhere:

'Adriatic Dusk' in *The Winnow* (Pushcart nominated)
'Apparition' in *After....*
'Bad Light' in *Sledgehammer*
'Bonfire night' in *Green Ink*
'China Blue' in *Marble*
'Concrete' in *Bad Lilies*
'Husband, this will be hard to hear' in *Atrium*
'In expectation of disappointment' in *Sledgehammer*
'Innismuirinn' in *Acropolis*
'Jane' in *Ink, Sweat & Tears* (voted 'poem of the month' for May 2020)
'Mammina proves the existence of god' in *Amethyst*
'Nine colours of my hometown' in *Long Poem Magazine*
'On perceiving new threat in the sky' in *Green ink*
'Perfect Trees' in *Dust*
'Polite Request' in *Dreich*
'She can't help herself' in *Twist in Time*
'Slow Progress' in *Capsule Stories*
'The end' in *Dreich*
'The science lesson' in *Dreich*
'To the shapeshifter' in *The Madrigal*
'Watermelon' in *Dreich*
'We all fell silent except for the men' in *Dust*
'Mother, the sun is trying to shine on me in' *Dust*

Contents

III

IV

V

Acknowledgements

My thanks to all those who have helped me bring *Relativism* to life: to Patrick Jamieson and the team at Taproot Press for seeing merit in the manuscript, and for devoting such time and attention to it; to Miranda Pearson for her careful reading of an earlier draft and for suggesting tweaks, many of which have been adopted in the final version; and to Mark Mechan of Red Axe Designs for creating the cover design with such skill. It has been a genuine pleasure to work with you all.

Thank you to my parents, Wes and Anne, to my brother, Wes, and to David—you all support me constantly in thousands of ways, big and small, and I am blessed to be able to depend on you. Thank you, Tom Neal, for lighting my life with your wisdom and kindness—I am privileged to be your Mum, and have a lot to learn from you. Thanks also to my poetry friends and encouragers (especially GB Clarkson, Zannah Kearns, Elizabeth Castillo, and many others on and offline), and to the many academic colleagues whose enthusiastic support for my parallel passion has been very much appreciated.

This book is dedicated to my mother Anne Ford with much love, and published on her birthday, in deep gratitude and thanks for the selfless support she has given me throughout my life. I have been incredibly fortunate in my family and friends, and most fortunate of all in having her.

A poem is a gesture toward home.
—Jericho Brown, 'Duplex'

I

Jane
For JCB

Jane shapes the town to herself.
Of the spire, the pond,
the iron bridge and the bandstand,
she is undoubted queen.

She cooks and eats. She feeds and clothes the world,
folding bodies and souls into comfortable communion.
She is a ladle, stirring.

She brings back treasures from sun-hardened places,
gives them up to the damp fingers of grass-stained children.
She is a shell haircomb.

She plays cards quickly. She smells of cocoa powder or of lilac
and vaporises priests with a raised eyebrow.
She is a raised eyebrow.

She hardly writes at all, but when she does
the lines she makes go through to the pages underneath.

She fixes herself to the spot; she pitches tents for the lost.
Are you lost?
She is a compass, pointing.

And then she moves away.

She moves away in all her beauty, in all her how-dare-yous.
She moves away in all her certainty, her life its own eloquence.
She moves away in all the crimson of our still-warm love for her.

Advice for firewalkers

All in this town must walk barefoot
on fire. Tangerine seethe beneath coal crackle.
Trial by ordeal, fever dream, cowardice
plucked out cleanly by the root.

At twilight, chanting—gentle at first—
threads through the streets, touching our terror
to its lips, the old gods stirring, remembering,
eager to do their worst.

The eggers-on seem unaware
that their own fire crouches, only bright thing
in a dank future. Fuel and spark now strangers,
but fated to meet and flare.

If you must walk on fire, then meet
it boldly. Light your own fire, let the embers burn
a long time, and walk, don't run. That way
the fire won't trouble you; you'll steal its heat.

Concrete

Sometimes it was ablaze with words and letters
IRA   PROVOS   FTP   gang names   and
WE'LL NEVER FORGET YOU BOBBY SANDS
along the bridge
in letters as tall as my dad.
Who was he?   I asked.
He was a man who killed himself.

But mostly it was spotless   equally happy
to sparkle in August sun or February frost
ringing under our skipping feet
tunnelling under the roads
and you would find
debris of adulthood down there
empty glue bags   broken bottles
crushed cigarette boxes
and things they said were snakeskins
and you must never touch   said dad
because as everyone knows
the skin of a snake is poisonous
and it never struck me as strange
that I never saw snakes about the place—
skins only.

The schools   the church   the library
pavements and paths
all my beginnings gleamed grey
my foundations
fixed.

I see less concrete now.

Asunder

During the day we were waterlilies and dancers, and at night
we were dolls, felted down and stitched into sleep.

However many ways I try to describe it, you'll never see it
because it's not yours, and that reminds me

how far we'll always be from one another. A distance
that affects us both, but that only I can feel.

And there you go, kinetic limbs, mouth stained with honey,
hands too full of life—you've grabbed

other people's shares as well as your own, not out of greed, but
only out of eager, thoughtless joy.

A Sorrowful Mystery

Not only a widow, she had also lost her eldest son. I knew him as a blurred photograph in a funeral booklet. My parents kept their copy in an atlas I could barely lift, his grainy face forever pressed against a map of Poland. She dressed in the deaths of the men she had loved, wound in veils and heavy coats even on warm days. Her memories walked before her when she left the house, a desolate procession that caused heads and voices to drop. She seemed to haunt our town rather than live in it. As her Polish friends died, or moved to be closer to children and grandchildren, she fell ever more silent. And when she crumpled during the Sorrowful Mysteries one morning after weekday Mass, no-one knew the youth who cradled her head in his lap and prayed over her in the rhythms of her girlhood as the veils fell away.

Family portrait in F-sharp minor

We don't talk much about guilt in this house
like we don't talk about oxygen molecules
or white blood cells or vital organs.
We talk a lot about fear
and how pointless it is.

We don't speak about how quickly time passes
but we sometimes mention the aquatic plants
whose Latin names I learned aged three
and how everything that's loved
is made eternal.

We don't fantasise about exotic places
or dream vacations, because we don't dream
of being anywhere but here. We talk about
how much we must have saved over the years
by staying where we are.

We don't discuss peace, but we talk a lot
about justice, and when we say justice
we mean our version. And when we talk
about love, which is all the time, it's understood
that love doesn't happen outside these walls.

Tides

Look carefully at the water, she says. Do you see
    how long a tide is? The tide is not only the noisy,
furious bit at the front; it stretches all the way
    back to the open sea. The loud bit, the bit that jumps
and shouts and tries to soak you is the bit you want
    to look at, of course. But look further back. See how
even as the front of the tide is hammering against
    the harbour wall, the same tide, further back,
is already quietly leaving? At first, it leaves to
    gather strength to come at us again. But eventually
it retreats and stays away. 'Retreats' means 'goes back',
    she says. This is the nature of tides. This is
what tides are: two things at once. Both
    a fierce, incoming force, full of drama and sensation—
feel it on your face, your tongue! It stings? Yes!
    That's the sting that tells you you're really here!
But at the same time it's a fading, departing thing.
    'Departing' is another word for leaving, she says.
She pushes my tumult of hair aside and cups her mittened
    hands around my cheeks—a salted peach in each palm.
It can't be any other way, she says. Remember this.

Cardiology

I never saw a heart without an arrow through it
till I was sixteen. Valentines, plush bears,
scribbles on jotter covers, desks, and walls,
casually-inflicted injuries on tree-trunks—
I thought all hearts came pre-wounded.

The boy behind the butcher's counter once showed me
a pig's heart, squat with fat, hoping I'd scream.
I was just puzzled— where was the arrow?
Clearly, it must only be human hearts
that come already pierced.

I had a chest x-ray once, and asked to see the image.
The woman smiled and said *we don't do that.*
Reporting the results, the doctor told me
everything seemed fine, so I assumed
my arrow must be in its proper place.

I used to move my shoulders in unnatural ways,
alert for any hint of gouging near my ribs.
Eventually, I realised we had to earn our wounds,
yet still I picture hearts as medieval martyrs—
skewered, but persevering.

Watermelon

When a watermelon appeared
among the shopping,
you knew it was a good day.
No-one who was angry
would think to bring home
an outsized, toylike,
cartoon-coloured thing,
a thing from a storybook
that lands on the counter
with a comedy bump
and opens with flamingo fanfare.
Once it was cracked and sliced
summer was underway,
and no-one could be angry
while actively engaged in summer,
eyes shut, gorging like ticks. No,
a watermelon was a ball of joy
and the joy was guaranteed
till it was done.

The Science Lesson

After the silence was over you led me
out of the heavy air tinged with sulphur
and threadbare beauty and into
a striplit room

where you still whispered as you talked
about mysteries of life and death
and guilt and karma
in laboratory language
in Latin names and numbers
in phrases I had heard on television

and suddenly the mind that raged and postured
worshipped experts.

I saw there was a fire in your brow
and you took my cold hand
and warmed it between your two large hands
with ostentatious care
and undue ceremony
but with strength enough
that I could feel your blood
coursing out of time with my faint pulse
only two skins away.

II

She never shuts her mouth

She hasn't shut her mouth in thirty years.
Was it the shock of the savage afternoon
that ripped this lifelong hole in her
or the power of the blast that blew her
off her feet and dumped her
in the road, bird-broken?

Was it the sight of half her young son's friend
blown into the street like a torn piece
of paper, eyes still bright?
His mouth gaping, like his body—
did hers open in silent answer
and forget to close again?

Or was it when she was told, much later
that her own warm boy was cold?
Did her lips part then to let
her sparrow of a soul escape?
For it did fly off to find and tend to him.

Or is it just that putting lips together
after all these years would feel
like a denial of the bodies, still and moving
plastered thick in dust and blood—
of ambulance doors swinging
of shopping bags abandoned in the road?

You should use eye cream

she says.
Mine's very good.
I'll show you the pot.

That's an unusual collar,
she says.
Is it supposed
to sit like that?

Is that normal Coke?
she says.
You know you feel much better
when you cut out sugar.

She says,
is that handbag definitely
black to match your shoes?
It looks navy in this light.

You need to be careful—
not everybody's as well-meaning as you.
You're so gullible,
she says,

when I tell her what I paid
for a coat on eBay.
They must have seen you coming.

Eyeliner's not for everyone,
she says,
while I'm wearing it,
it can make some people's eyes look
piggy.

She says,
you have terrible taste
in men. I don't know why
you let them muck you around.

You should stand up for yourself,
she says.
I don't know why
you have such low self-esteem.

Exam conditions

She looks bewildered by my replies.

Why don't they have gentle lamps in rooms like this?

One thing I do remember is that I drank far more than I
normally would. She frowns: wrong answer.

I'm not allowed a drink of water right away, but that isn't the
worst thing about all of this.

I'm not sure I'll *ever* remember the details.

The doctor is talking about swabs.

How did I get here? Oh yes, that's right.

I surprise myself by thinking how important it is not to
misrepresent; to be fair to him.

The overhead lights are scouring me down to the steel.
(I know not to say this out loud.)

She's asking me to think carefully now.

This isn't consensual. *This* isn't consensual.

The only person who can make this better is my mother.
Where is she? Oh yes, that's right.

I try to explain: it's like the way you can't see things when they're
held too close to your face.

The doctor is asking *was it consensual?*

Somehow I'm breathing unassisted.

They're going to look for illegal drugs in my system.
They'll find them.

Slow progress

The others were fast—
dry, crackling, quick.
They ignited at the first spark,
flared up and were gone.
I, being slower, lagged behind,

struggling to be alight, unable
to catch fire, though everything
around me was consumed,
until at last, tragedy lost patience
and moved on.

And now I make a patchwork of myself.
A patch for each of them:
all patches, Frankenlife.
I draw breath after breath
of their unclaimed air
and it scorches my paper throat,
incinerates my tinder lungs.

At last, I find a way to burn.

Mother, the sun is trying to shine on me

again, as you said it would.
I've kept the windows shuttered as you told me to, but
hot fingers always find ways through.

The sun is saying it might turn me golden if I step outside.
But 'might' was never good enough for you
and won't be good enough for me

and I'm remembering everything you've said
about how ballerina skin like mine
is slipper-soft, and cannot be exposed.

I think the sun might be a liar, Mother.
You tell me that I mustn't melt—
that I'm a fool to think I could be golden.

I move the slats a little
see some slow, sun-softened people
and I cannot help but notice that not one of them is burnt.

What should I do? Tell me again
and quickly, Mother. My hand is on the handle
and it's nearly noon, when shade is hard to find.

Mammina proves the existence of God

The day is on its hands and knees. Mammina basks
on the balcony in great-grandmother dignity
in all the quiet of a woman who has outlived her daughter,
collarbones glistening, little cross flashing pink
and gold among rivulets of August evening sweat
as the sun finally loses its grip and goes down fighting,
painting the duomo in eyeshadow colours.
The whole horizon is made of churches.

An ambulance squeals along an unseen street,
not the smooth wail of the ambulances back home,
but a desperate, discombobulated sound like the cry
of a confused animal. Mammina makes the sign of the cross,
lets loose a fast prayer. Her words are a string
of small, round beads, tumbling one after the other.

How can you be so sure anyone is listening? I ask
in her bubbling tongue. My head is dusky with
the sweetness the city gives off at the height of summer,
and with all my days and nights at university.

Mammina opens one eye, closes it, smiles back in her chair,
takes a fat medjool date between leathery thumb and
forefinger, squeezes it lightly, and says

This perfect thing does not exist by accident.

Memento

I keep a scrap of the horror in my pocket
a few square centimetres of molten metal
that winked & caught my eye when I went back to visit
the hole. I rub it between my thumb and forefinger
~~compulsively, like praying the Rosary~~
occasionally, to remind me
that the house isn't there anymore
and there's no point going back.

I shouldn't have gone back even once, because
I like to think of what happened as
~~performance art / an afternoon play~~
a dream I'm about to wake up from
and that's much easier
when you're not staring into a charred crater
and smelling ~~your decomposing future~~ melted pavement.

There was another just three weeks after ours—
a cafeteria at lunchtime.
No-one was killed this time, the news reporter said
~~so it barely merits a mention on the bulletin~~
and my mother and grandmother sang *Thank God*
so when I read later that a young woman
had both her legs blown off, and a boy was blinded
~~I knew that God had finally shaken off the dust of us.~~
I didn't like to tell them.

I went back again, and kept going till they cleared the site.
You'd have hated the memorial garden. Can you believe
they inscribed your precious name up there among
~~the tacky fake flowers in implausible political colours~~
the tributes without asking?
I'd slip my Walkman around my neck
~~like a ligature~~ and under my coat
and I'd play it over and over again, the tune that never fails
~~to bring you back from the dead~~ to get me humming

and we'd sway together drowsily
in the corner of the crater I thought must be the room
where you told me ~~you hated this town~~
I smelt like peace, faintly floral
where you told me ~~it should be razed without mercy~~
you loved whiskey and me, in that order, laughing gently
at your own audacity

where you told me that you barely heard the Nonsense
in the streets anymore, because the sound
of our future rushing toward us was too loud
and *Let it consume us* you said *Let it engulf us completely.*

Adriatic Dusk

I turn the paint-tin, catch sight of the label—
the memory sits me down, abruptly, on the stairs.
I'm at a table in the mountains outside Mostar
hazy blue laughter
and the merest hint of sea.

The dusk's a periwinkle shawl around my shoulders.
Tomatoes the size of my palms, meals in themselves.
The table-water sweet, somehow. Olives
which I do not like at home
have no bitterness here.

Plum-sized grapes hang overhead—we pluck
and eat them. We should wash them, but unusually
we're reckless. Surely no germ can sicken us here
in the violet time
where nature is suspended?

Just look at the sky now, raging mauve.
It's nearly midnight, yet we sit outdoors, defiant
for this is a place where the veil is often open
and creatures know
and heaven bends down.

Tomorrow I'll be leaving, and I'll cry soon for this place
but I'll stow these blues and purples in my luggage
and I'll paint my hallway *Adriatic Dusk* one day
after the war
in twenty years from now.

III

How I Didn't Meet Your Father

There was this one man who
wanted to marry me, but who,
when I told him I was late, said
if the worst comes to the worst
it's probably better if you get rid of it
because of where we are in our careers.
And suddenly

the Earth was not a home, a green thing,
but a planet, a blue thing,
a scientific thing,
an orb in a void,
and I was a crouched creature sitting small
on its surface,
cold in space,
listening to a song being played in the distance.
And I knew in this moment

that I could never marry this man,
because he would eat my children and me
and not even notice he had done it,
and because although (as it turned out)
you didn't exist yet, I knew I could never
forgive him for calling you *the worst*.

The mother line

You're part angel, he says, his finger pad
travelling along the stroke of my cheekbone.
Well yes, I smile to myself, shoulder blades tingling—
but it was very long ago, and by now
very diluted.

My mother was more angel than me, and
her mother more than her. There are no photographs
of the mothers before that, but if there were
I know it would beat stronger
with each step back.

Years later, when I hold my brand new girl
older ladies with velvet cheeks and aquamarine eyes
lean in knowingly and say she's an angel
and one meets my eye and says
I knew your mother.

My mother's pronoun was not 'it'

After Michael Conley, 'An Otherwise Uneventful Holiday'

My mother was iridescent
soft with a sting
and although (naturally) she didn't have a heart
she loved all 40,000 of us equally.
Human scientists have observed that
'once the adult female jellyfish
has released its eggs into the water
it provides no further care for its young.'

Well, that's a lie.
We were family. I'm sorry to dispute
the authority of human science
but I was there.
She'd take us swimming in the Aegean—
has *your* mother ever done that?
And she'd sing us to sleep with a great tenderness
completely inaudible to human scientists.
Then, because she loved us oh-so-much
she let us go.

I wish you could have seen my mother
in her element, the embodiment of grace—
not as she was at the end
a blob on the sand, drying out
under hostile, unseeing eyes.
I wish you all a mother capable
of giving so much life, and in return
asking only to swim, and swim.

Given to Worrying

'She's given to worrying', they say. I imagine a ceremony soon after her birth. The girl child sleeping, powder-soft and small in wool and cotton; the parents milk-faced, sombre, holding her up and out in offering; and the iron god Worrying, resplendent on colossal marble throne, indolently blinking between huge looping horns, accepting the sacrifice with indifference.

As she grows, she is told: 'You are given to Worrying.' She accepts this. What else is there? She knows of others in her family who were also singled-out. She accepts that for her there will be silver, not gold. There will be grey, blue, black and white, and only occasional flashes of pink or green. She submits to nocturnality, to early wrinkles; concedes that the hours between twilight and dawn will trap her away from reason, open a chasm between her and those not given to Worrying. She understands that she will never lie carefree in a lover's arms while the night shifts its shades on her bedroom wall.

She forewarns those she meets, 'I'm given to Worrying,' giving notice of the limits on what others can expect. She might not have a child—best not, as she is *so* given to Worrying—or she might, in which case he will doubtless be offered up too. For Worrying is a greedy god, always ravenous, though he feasts deeply, voraciously, all night, every night.

In expectation of disappointment

I've decided not to love you, just in case
you leave like the others.

I believed in their permanence, but
they slipped through me
like ghosts, like sand through
a desperate fishing net, as though I
were made of nothing at all, and they left

nothing behind
but a chill streak of fear
and a distrust of all who are like them.

And you are just like them.

One left in the night, woke me up
as he left. He left me bloodied.
Another waited until I had made
public declarations—of love, I suppose—

and then left, and I had to tell everyone
that no, I wouldn't be introducing him,
that he hadn't stayed, that there would be
no pictures of us together, no events,
no shared life. And their faces!

Their pitying faces. So please, forgive me

if I don't show the murky hospital photos,
if I buy nothing, prepare nothing
(except my body for the blow),
if I don't name you, and try not to love you
until I know you won't leave
like the others.

Schrödinger's daughter

Tabitha, I never knew you.
You vanished on the day my son was born.
Seconds before they dragged him free
you winked and arched and stretched
and said goodbye.

You knew the score—
that when the box was opened
just one version could be there.

Only ever one shape on the screen
but I sensed both—
my pulsing son and his spectral sister
cat-curled in quantum dark together
purring there
twin-tight.

But what becomes of those who don't survive
the interaction with outside?
And what decides which one will disappear
and which will stay?

It must have been some subatomic thought
or poisoned wish of mine that did for you—
selected him, and sent you off
a stray.

Sapling

I'm remembering the day we planted it.
You, picturing the monumental larches
that fringed your childhood garden,
though you knew this wasn't a larch;
me, imagining the towering elm
in the park opposite my teenage home,
though I knew this wasn't an elm.

When we went our not-quite-separate ways
I inherited our Eden and its thickening tree,
and now I find it growing unpredictably.
I'm wondering if we planted it too close
to the windows—it seems sometimes
to steal light from my evenings—
and I worry, though not often,
that in time its roots might reach across
and tear the house from under me.

But I'm looking out of the window now,
and you should see it, oh sweetheart,
you should see it, trembling
as though it could hear me think,
and shaking out splendour over everything.

When he goes into orbit I stop breathing

as though I've transferred all my oxygen to him
to use up there   and in return he's given me
a piece of outer space   just big enough for one
and I'll inhabit it   till he returns
lips pursed   breath held   unblinking
my chest won't move   until he splashes down again.

I fear for him   up there in silver-studded darkness
between night and day   precious existence suspended
on flimsy threads of human understanding   up against
all the great unknowns   fierce forces for which
whole planets   suns and galaxies   are throwaway
need not exist   might disappear   can go to Hell.

My shred.   My poor frail carbon-based life-form.
I know you'd find it natural
to slip your tether   suffocate   and drift away.

Not breathing   I stand by my dashboard   adjusting dials
checking screens   listening for beeps and pulses just in case
he's out there somewhere trying to crackle through to me.
He's never tried before   but if he did   I'd want
to offer him my voice immediately   to reassure him that
his home is waiting warm for him   whenever he might land.

Each time   through space   through breathlessness
I keep hold of his hand.

IV

On perceiving a new threat in the sky

Darling. The evenings shorten and draw in.
Is your clock not as punctual as mine?
You stroll through days as though each hour were two,
and stop at each new gate for friendly words.
Can you not see the thickening of the sky
and that each morning creeps in later now?

I'm sure the air's a degree cooler now
(but let me take some time to choose my words)
and this, to me, looks like a spiteful sky—
see how the crows seek shelter from it too?
I wonder if it's time to go back in,
seek sanctuary for your soul and mine?

I know your outlook's sunnier than mine
and that your tendency is always to
focus on now, not what may come, and in
a way, I envy you. But thoughts of now
will not suffice for long. In other words,
you need to pay attention to the sky.

Look up, and tell me this is not our sky—
they're not our clouds that gather and roll in.
If, hand on heart, you'll soothe me with these words,
I'll quickly fold your weathered hand in mine
and promise to stop speaking of it now,
and say I feel the heat of summer too.

Let's walk together aimlessly down to
the gate, wait till the amber fills the sky
then turn for home, our thoughts engrossed in now—
in how my roots are thoroughly dug in
to your soil, and your roots dug into mine—
and let's be economical with words.

But how do you suppose that we, with words
or lack of words, can stem the coming Now
that seeps around your corner, around mine,
that glowers there above us in the sky,
that, ever more insistent, warns us to
take note? The evenings shorten and draw in.

The brightness in your tone can't undermine
this stealthy dread, too shadowy for words:
feel how the low sky draws around us now.

Escapology

It's during your third hospitalisation that you take on the look
of someone trapped inside himself, and I begin to wonder
for the first time if my magic isn't working.

I saw a trick once where a man was sealed in a locked box
and the box lowered to the bottom of the sea, and he was down there
for so long that some people wandered off, shaking their heads.

A woman who has recently been to the hairdressers takes me
out to the corridor and tells me, patiently but firmly, to adjust
my expectations. I pretend to listen, but am burningly aware

that she will go home that evening to a healthy husband.
Perhaps one who has dinner waiting. Perhaps one who'll watch
a film with her and then put the bins out before bed.

On the shore, people began to cry. Children were led away.
Many couldn't look, but after what seemed an impossible time
a shout went up: he had broken the surface.

I understand why your face and abdomen are swollen, and
why you've begun to yellow like my old notes, but
I don't understand why your limbs are so smooth and pale

and thin, no-one has explained that, and though I'd like
to know, I want them to hear me asking the right questions about
the important things. Nothing superficial.

I saw a trick once where a girl had done everything she could to make you happy. He doesn't drink because he's unhappy *the patient woman says. But my eyes are fixed on the surface.*

Perfect trees

We'd drive around.
We'd drive around and look
for perfect trees, turning one way or another,
toward beauty or away from it, we didn't know—
deciding which direction felt most promising, most likely
to reward us with a glimpse of perfection.

We'd consider the composition
of a perfect tree—what elements,
what proportions—and discuss these things
in detail, very calmly, though you resented me,
and always agreeing, though our other conversations
flared red and made me run away.

We'd drive around in search
of sudden beauty, always agreeing
when we found a perfect tree, but never
photographing it—we didn't want to flatten it.
We'd try instead to remember how we found it,
though we never returned.

Husband, this will be hard to hear

but you're dead, and I hate your ghost.

You died in such small increments that I think
you may have missed your own last breath, but even so,
it was no less the shock to me. Fetal with grief,
I felt such eiderdown relief that anything of you remained
that I encouraged him to hang around, a charm against
the solitude that seemed to seep in under every door.
I thought it might be a bit like having a cat. But
it's nothing like having a cat.

The blow was realising that he's really nothing like you,
darling, he's cold, and when he slides between the sheets
at night I inch away. OK, I more than inch—
I now sleep in a different room, with lights on, and
he sleeps in what was formerly our bed.
I've steadily yielded whole rooms to him, but still,
somehow, he's always in my way.

I tried with him, truly I did—
I crept from my sleepless room
to ice myself beside him two or three times, but
he was never hungry, like you.
Eventually I remembered that, of course,
ghosts never are.

Worse still, he does some things that frankly creep me out—
the crawling, the shapeshifting.
And this will be the hardest thing of all for you to hear—
your dog detests him too. I'm sorry,
sweetheart, but you always had two rules:

We must be honest with each other.

And,

We don't involve the dog in our delusions. It has its own life.

The first of these applies, I think, and so,
although this must be very hard to hear,
I knew you'd want to know.

Polite request

I would be grateful if you would pretend
to be distracted by a programme
on TV, or by the pages of a book,
and fail to hear the closing of the door,
or see I have the large suitcase with me,
or, if you do, resist the urge to look.

I left the fridge and cupboards fully stocked.
I left your laundry folded on the bed.
I left the rings relaxing on the shelf
where, like me, I know you won't miss them.
Now, it's time to shake this sense of being bereft,
and face the wind, and reckon with myself.

She can't help herself

She's smiling
 the woman whose husband
 will shortly have her murdered
  whose thimble, whose sheets
 whose husband's flesh
  will soon be warmed
  by a more obliging body
 with a lot more give
and quite a bit less to say.

She's smiling
 and at my leisure I can appraise
 every detail of her face, but
  the only gaze here is hers
 and when I meet her eyes, I know
  that I am on her turf
  and she keeps her eyes on me
 and she keeps her real name
on a rope around her neck.

I feel her steel.

They say her wit was like a blade
 perhaps she smiled too much
 and lacked a blind eye
  perhaps she should have saved her tongue
 for flattery and prayers

but this is what survives of her
this, her last laugh
And as I finally turn my back, she says

You must understand—
a sharp girl can play sweet, but not for long.

V

DECOMPOSER

not a looker
not one of the pastel ones
the frilly ones   i don't evoke
a fairytale

not one of the coloratura trilly ones
unornamented   i lack

the glockenspiel magic
of the bell-like ones

the opera crescendo
of the ones like open wounds

the melodrama of
the cymbal discs that crash
along the trunks of trees

humble member of the chorus
monophonic underhum
brown vibrato low note
bass humdrum

and i'll have you all   in the end.

the family strolling past andante
their falsetto boy   his freckled friend

they bring their faces close in
for a front stalls view   mimic retching
and trample on   flattening
the fiddleheads

the couple fugally entwined
their dog that sniffs around me for a second
dropping cords of drool

i'll have them all   in the end.

knuckled thumb of a thing
perfectly pitched here
i mind my business   but
i'm a great believer in the equal value
of every part

so come

come to me   all you who are
busy   overplayed   out of tune
you with the symphonic inner life
you who have agonised over the meaning
of a look   or a word

come to me   you whose skull
houses libraries   you who recite homer
in the original greek   and baudelaire

in french   you who can name

the most important european artists
of the inter-war years   and recognise their work on sight
you who can discourse   as an equal
with professors of poetry on matters of
enjambment   tone   and metre

you whose synapses
fire fast enough to calculate
the derivative of y (with respect to x)
without pencil and paper   come to me

you who can name any beethoven sonata in one bar
who have seen the sun set over
the adriatic   the aegean   the south china sea

you who have slept
in a tree house in kenya
on a yacht moored on the riviera
in a studio in paris
in a squat in mile end

you with the sharp jawline   the flat stomach
the natural beauty   you
with the well-tempered clavicle
the well-turned ankle   the excellent eye for detail

so much bone and jelly.

come to me   and   with perfect timing

i will give you   rest.

Pearls & swine

'If I come back,' you say
'I want to be a pearl bracelet
owned by a woman who loves to keep me warm.
So rosy for me that she'll never take me off.
Not even when she lets some swine get lucky with her.
Not even afterwards in the bath.
Pearls should be fine in water, she'll say.
And she'll lie back, pig-pink in hot water
and finger me, and me,
I'll be all lustre.'

to the shapeshifter

you might be a melting clock   but you are
a man with a dog's head.   beneath your muzzle   your tie
is pale orange silk   and your jacket
is forest green tweed.   you hold a pipe in your hand
which you never raise to your lips.
the thing is just to stand there.
you only stand on scuffed parquet floors   in front of
whitewashed walls.   you might be framed
but it's not necessary.

you could have been a high-backed chair   but in fact
you are a turquoise tiled fireplace   clashing gently with
an exposed brick wall.
you don't like the heat   but it's your vocation
and you suck it up.   very dated
you'd hoped they might rip you out
but you grew on them.   they're quirky.

you always said the life force was in everything
and look at you now   member of the inanimate community
yellow Bakelite coffee pot   revelling in caffeinated rightness.
i'd have recognised you anywhere.   on reflection
i'd have expected something else   perhaps a rubber duck
or a jack-in-the-box   but this is perfect for you
bravo   you lucked out.
first thing anyone sees in the room
and bound to be touched and held.

Nine colours of my hometown

I. *A collective madness*

A neighbour once told me of a period
when the people of this town lost their minds
and began naming their daughters using
jewel-toned words like Envy, Heresy, and Vanity,
but the sons still had good earth-coloured names.
This was around the same time
that some kings were made of glass.

II. *A plan*

When I hear news of your death
—it may be years after the event—
I will sink to the floor.
I've already planned which corner
of which room I'll use,
and what I'll be wearing (vermillion).
I hope not to be in the house alone,
because I would prefer a witness.
If I am in the house alone, I will wait
and pretend to hear the news later
when someone is there to observe.

III. *A gaoler*

I was once locked up with a woman
    who did everything for me
and did it exceptionally well, but who accused me
    of being imprisoned willingly—
she said it every ten minutes, with her petrol eyes.
    She also said
be careful who you love
    she said
better still, don't love anyone
as none of them is me.
    All this she said solely with eye movements
and a flat, unmoving face.

IV. *A confusion*

There was a man among us once who seemed to be a light source, and we allowed ourselves to hope because of him, but he became caught, somehow, in a grey-blue confusion, and like a sheep in a hedge could not seem to escape it. He/the confusion (they were now as one) became like a beacon attracting various kinds of sorrow to our people, so we had to send him away from us, still tangled in his confusion, and we sang sorrowful songs to him as he went. There was a moment of stillness when he disappeared from view, and women wept; but things quickly returned to the way they had been, except that from now on, we would be less ready to hope.

V. *A companionship*

Unexpectedly, on an olive-green day, Resentment came and visited me, and she was not as ugly as I had been led to believe. She befriended me, and we grew to know one another; we took lunches together outdoors in the shady part of the garden, and found we liked the same herbs. We sat side by side in the evenings, slowly reshaping, each to the other. And I don't remember which of us suggested that we should live together from now on, but that is what happened. She is here right now.

VI. *A retelling*

To summarise, this is what we come from—nothing.
All the patterns on my sofas and plates
and all the oven smells of my family's teatimes—
these were illusions.
All the cartoon delight of hundreds of birthdays
and school holidays.
All the jarring of my bones and the bursting of my heart
as my school shoes bounced over open-plan gardens
and tarmac paths
and echoed through concrete underpasses.
All the love between us, in the end that's what it was—
a grass-green nothing.
But our nothing was half-mad with joy.

VII. *A confession*

Death has moved in, and is making itself at home in you. I'm sorry to say it was the first thing I noticed when I saw you today—your mouth chewing nothing, your eyes darting, all wickedness and twinkling gone. There is a chalky pleadingness about you now, as your mind flies, doing rewrites.

Et ego te absolvo a peccatis tuis.

VIII. *A bedtime story*

Stop asking me for wisdom—
I have little enough for myself.
And stop asking for stories of our people—
our people were not always in the right,
and I am tired,
and my sorrow is the shape of his absence.

I can only tell you what I know,
and all I know
is that life is a soft, apricot thing
that takes its own duration to ripen,
so that you never enjoy the ripening.

I'm sorry if I've put that bluntly,
but I am tired.

IX. *An escape attempt*

And if you should give gravity the slip and start
to rise up as though air-filled, you can be sure
    I'll become a piece of the pavement.
I'll grab your ankle
and pull down with all my grim graphite weight—
    this town is not yours to shrug off like a coat.

Bad light

I'm in the mood to listen
so he moves his head closer
to mine, and he's an artist, and he's telling me
that there's no such thing as bad light
and that robots can never be artists
on account of the need for a soul
but he's also a poet, and he says that all poetry
is war poetry, and I'm certain that a moment ago he also said
that all desire is really mourning
so he must be a philosopher too
and I'll go along with all of his generalisations
because I'll never be held
to them, and my body is the Earth
rotating on its axis and travelling around the sun
and my head is an attic, where only a few
shafts of light cut in around the shutters
picking out the scratches and grease stains on the floorboards
and I don't care what he says
this light is bad.

VI

Late lunch

We're eating a late lunch together in a little place
where you know the owner, and the waitress when she
takes our drinks order seems a shade proprietorial, and
although we've chosen a table deep inside, as far away
from doors and windows as possible, still the sun
has found us out, has found a way to slice in sharply
across our faces, making us peer directly at each other
instead of our usual half-glances, and we're discussing
a celebrated writer who did his best work in the 1950s,
and who was married to another writer who did
her own best work in the 80s, once the Great Man had died,
and the words I'm permitting to leave my mouth
are about this couple, performing the kind of veneration
that you seem to require from me, but secretly I regard them
as the kind of people I certainly wouldn't want to meet
in real life, they've always seemed to me to be
as bad as each other, but at the same time I'm quietly
envying them their unhappy but important life together,
a life recorded and admired, a life with bone structure, and most
of all a joint life, and all of this is what my words
are officially saying and concealing, but what I'm also doing,
by sitting here and looking straight at you and having this
inconsequential conversation is telling you the truth,
and the truth is that you are more myself than my nail-beds
or the roots of my hair, and it is also true that although to you I
may look like someone capable of great happiness
and abandon, I am not, as a matter of fact I was

both assassin and gravedigger to my own joy, I carefully
took its pulse before throwing in the first shovel of dirt,
just to make certain that I had left no flutter of life,
and this was some time ago now, and I must surely be close
to getting used to it, and although I feel convinced that
I cannot endure a life in which we don't belong to each other,
I also know that I will.

Apparition
For Mary Oliver, after 'Wild Geese'

And when I sense that I am in a state of grace
She appears, and moves toward me, fresh
In white cotton trousers and blue waterproof jacket
And I know three things, immediately:
    She is young.
        She is perfectly content.
            She is of the sea.

We sit together, side by side on a slope
High above the city, looking to the North
To the devastating North
As the last of the light leaves
And a storm muscles in, gull-grey.

I sense that it is time to ask my question, so
I turn to her and say

      Mother Mary, are you sure
      That I do not have to be good
      And spend my life repenting on my knees?

And though she is young tonight
She understands my question about the words
She will not write for years.

And she speaks in my mother's voice
(Which of course she didn't have)
And instead of answering my question
She says

I can see that you have never loved anyone properly.

  But are you sure? I say.
  About the goodness and repentance:
  Are you sure?

Child, she says
(She's younger than me)

Soft animal child
Why do you need to be sure?

I realise, or possibly decide

That there is nothing wrong with wanting to be safe.

That my demon doesn't know it's chasing me.

That darkness doesn't hide things as well as light.

That I am able to love even the ugliest bodies.

That the heart, like the eye, loves symmetry.

That grief, the unwinnable kind, is coming for both of us:

that mine will be vast and ragged, a mountain range;

that yours will be interplanetary-quiet.

That abandoned things become wild and beautiful.

That I can no longer live inside this sadness.

That I can no longer live inside this sadness.

How to be free

Never have a lover who's too magical to leave,
who tears at your guts and throws you off balance.
Don't marry a spouse who takes faultless care of you.
Never take a job that pays too well.
Don't live in a house that breathes in time with you,
that hums too perfectly in tune with you, or is
too heavy with love to sell.
Don't own too many books you long to read again.
Let there be nowhere that feels as though you grew up through
the cracks in its pavements, a place you need
to be buried in.
Never have a child.

We all fell silent except for the men

their solemn mahogany baritones closing around
a keening гармошка,[1] deepening, swelling, snaking

between us, causing our skins to shed, winding
around the hissing braziers, and it was as though

all the longing in the earth's bones sprouted, serpentine,
charmed from sleep by Russian chords, and I decided

just to dissolve into this longing, this sinuous lament,
this отравление,[2] uncoil myself from the hold of home,

of language, of all my loves, and from now on
my home would be this poison-apple moment,

my language a dirge rich with consonants,
and my only loves would be

милый,[3] любимый,[4] Ангел мой.[5]

---

1 *Garmoshka*, a Russian accordion.

2 *Atravleniye*, intoxication or poisoning.

3 *Milyi*, darling.

4 *Lyubimiy*, beloved.

5 *Angel moy*, my angel.

China blue

A false move. Her blue mug
in pieces on the flagstones.

Scanning the brokenness, I see
it's hopeless, a perfect shattering.

Some is powder. How instantly
things become irretrievable. How suddenly

the noise stopped, and here we are.
She sipped from it only this morning

and I noticed that she turned it, held it
to the light admiringly, and traced

the floral pattern with her finger. China blue,
her favourite colour. A sliver of beauty

in each of her mornings, I know it was precious to her,
and I know that she'll deny this now.

Pentecost

Sometimes   when lips are forced apart in grief   or fear

a bird flies in and mates with you   for life.

Bonbon head on pillow chest

this bird is perfect peace

a peace that wasn't won   so can't be lost.

A peace for the ages   a peace sufficient

unto the day   has chosen you.

There is no why   nor anything to do

but be a gentle host.

Trying to forget is remembering

a contradiction, just as trying to sleep is a conscious thing. When sleep washes in of its own accord, grip softens. The book drops at the side of the armchair. The floppy fingers of a dreaming child will easily release a close-clasped treasure. In the same way, time will coax the mind to loosen its hold on olden things, to hand over out-of-date sweetness and sour. It will be as gentle as falling asleep. So there's no use trying—the mind will let go in its own time. Until then, let your grasp be tender—remember, they are old.

When you hear the word 'home'

your inner screen will flicker silently with many images, but I want the largest and brightest of them to be images of me at my best. And when you think of what might be happening at home I want you to picture me dropping bags and shoes in a broad hallway, entering an orderly kitchen, and turning on a tap. And when you are homesick, I need your suffering to be caused by the fact that you are not currently (i) telling me something about a film, or a song, or a book, while also (ii) noticing that my hands look honest, and (iii) smiling because my eyelashes resting on my cheek remind you of a tiny caterpillar you found sitting on a downy leaf in a rubbish-strewn flowerbed when you were eight years old and already beyond everyone and everything. And when you imagine coming home, I want you to be imagining my honest-looking hands spread wide across your back, collecting you up, drawing you the last few centimetres of the way, pressing you home. And if all of this is the case, you can be anywhere, and I will be fine.

VII

Innismuirinn

It takes all night to row there, and the fear hangs around me like an anchor, but I can no longer go without knowing, so I work my arms and legs till muscle threatens to peel from bone, slip over the side, and swim away. The cave is on the island's farthest shore, so even when the shoulders of the land appear, there's still a way to go. Like all from Mullaghveagh, I've known the legend since I was a girl. A sea-cave famous for its echo, and Muirinn, long ago, who became distressed when her beloved moved away and left her, followed by all of her relations, one by one. In deep sorrow, the story goes, she rowed out to the cave to hide, and only when the darkness gave no answer in return for her lamentations did she realise that she'd been dead for decades. And once you've understood, the legend says, your soul departs. The island bears her name now, and whole boatloads of tourists sail there and back in an afternoon, snacking all the way, for a chance to send their noise ricocheting around the ancient walls, obliging the noble stone to respond in kind. Sometimes they hurl profanities; I've seen it on their viral videos, and I hate them for it. I can hardly feel my body now, and I wonder if I'm numb with exhaustion, or if I have my answer already. I've decided that when I get there, I won't shout 'Hello!'—the walls have been greeted enough. Instead of shouting, I'll sing. A lullaby, so that if nothing comes back, the last thing I'll ever hear will be sweet.

Rock song

It's a small stretch of sea, but it boils with anger. Still,
it will be the colour of my family's eyes, so
however much it rants, it can put no fear in me.
And the journey will take no time at all, and I will be
the only passenger, and unafraid of being alone,
although I am no sailor. And when I step off at the other side
the stones will clamour around my feet, singing:

> *Our little wee girl, our fair one,*
> *Our lost princess, our own true love,*
> *We knew you'd end up here.*

I'll reply that it was never in any doubt,
for where else could I finally be, but here in this place
where the stones are moulded perfectly to my feet,
and the clouds sit snugly around my shoulders,
and the bullets fit perfectly between my eyes?

And I'll tell them how I haven't slept
in all the time I've been away, that I've never found
anywhere that feels enough like home to dream in,
and that I've lain and listened while their song's fingers
reached across the sea and stroked my whitening hair.
And the stones will answer:

But how can that be, wee girl, wee love,
How can you not have slept for a hundred years?
And do you know what they've been doing to us
While you were gone? It would break your heart,
You'd die of it.

I'll reply that I'm here now, am I not?
And that no harm will come to them. And I'll ask them
to make it so that nothing can ever remove me.
And the stones will sing:

Thank you, thank you, don't ever leave again.

And I will promise not to, and in one simple movement
we will become each other, as it should always have been—
after all the exile, how easy it will be in the end,
me turning to stone and the stones taking the shape
of a song-stricken girl, salt-blasted
and ocean-eyed, but home now,
and made monument.

Olding

We are olding now, and you've gone home
to rest, and I'll stay here, warm in the copper
and the gold a while, but soon
like chairs after a concert
like hands of cards after a lively game
like tents after the circus
we will fold.

A man with a brush will come to sweep the dregs
and no-one and nothing will roll up
but our flags
and our corners
and our trouser legs
for we are old.

But there is colour in us yet, and so
let us identify the sacred ones
and love them
and be gentle with the rest
for we are going
and we cannot help but go.

Diminuendo

I wonder which word I'll lose next.
Yesterday, I lost two. One beginning with *h*

or possibly *s*

a word for a very high sort of shoe,
a kind I never wore, and it wasn't a word
I'd have needed very often,
but when I went looking for it yesterday
it wasn't where I'd left it.

Never mind.

The other was a word I'm sure began with *d*
a musical term,
the opposite of *crescendo*, so
I suppose it must mean *gradually becoming quieter*.

Like me.

I'm sad about this one. ~~An innuendo?~~
I used to play—
the name of the instrument
escapes me for the moment—a giant violin
that you sit down with. ~~Umbrella? Cherry?~~

Never mind,

the problem is
that losing musical language feels
like losing inches off my height.
Like taking off a pair of…

                      …high-heeled shoes.

~~A demolition.~~
~~A demotion.~~
~~A dimension.~~

                      It lessens me.

Care Plan
For JB

She said that starving was a gentle death,
the woman making plans for future care.
she said they'd need to summon up the strength
to let him hunger, waste and wither there.

The woman making plans for future care
told them the time had come to let him go.
To let him hunger, waste and wither there,
and do all this without unseemly show.

She said the time had come to let him go,
and took a sip of water from her glass
without unseemly show, but still it seemed,
like the untouched plate of biscuits, rather crass.

She took a sip of water from her glass
and stirred the cooling coffee in her cup.
The plate of biscuits sat, untouched and crass.
She checked her watch: best start to sum things up.

Stirring the cooling coffee in her cup,
she smiled. Her smile contained no trace of doubt.
She checked her watch again—*To sum things up,
she said, it's better not to drag things out.*

She smiled a smile that held no trace of doubt
and ushered them toward the open door.
She thought it better not to drag things out—
she had to beat the traffic, leave by four.

Ushering them through the open door,
she knew her diary couldn't overrun.
She had to beat the traffic, leave by four,
so had to close this meeting down by one.

She couldn't let her diary overrun—
the restaurant was booked for half-past eight.
Unless she closed this meeting down by one,
her partner and their friends would have to wait.

The restaurant was booked for half-past eight.
She said that starving was a gentle death.
Her partner and their friends would have to wait.
She knew that they would summon up the strength.

*

Elegy before time

We only ever have as long as it takes for one express train
to pass another, a violent grab of time
and lacking stillness. It's brief, and blasted, but we'll take it.

Wanting more, of course. Isn't that our condition?
If we had all we longed for, would we
still want it? Would 'wanting' mean anything at all?

I think I know the thrust of what the doctor told you, but
the fingers of your silence are on my lips.
If I could speak, the only thing I'd say would be

Don't forget me. Which is too little, and the wrong way round.
But you have always been the lake, and I the drop.
Here's stillness. Have we both stopped breathing already?

The back of three

A ball rolls left to right across the path.
A dog barks in the next-door house but one.
A sudden blast of wind buffets the grass.

A woman tugs a rain-hood from her bag.
An iron cloud plugs the last weak shaft of sun.
The hours from noon till tea-time always drag.

A cat across the way has caught a bird.
I turn my head until it's not alive.
You died three weeks ago, and I've just heard.

A boy retrieves the ball, calls to his friend.
The weatherman said maybe rain by five.
The day turned out quite bitter, in the end.

The End

I'd push the sun back down if I could.
No more days, please—while she sleeps
we all will sleep; the world will sleep
or end, I couldn't care.

Now an echo of banal conversation
resounds through the hallway, through the thick wall
of my room, through three decades,
determined to be heard.

Come in here and get those wet things off. Don't put that there!

The sense of being cheated overwhelms.

A boy is crying in my arms. He doesn't know
the half of it, the giant aeonic rupture
of our loss. And as I smooth his hair and lie to him
I picture a mountain finally working loose,
crashing into a lake; filling it.

And those who pass here centuries from now will say
apparently, this was all once underwater.